Sassy Sips & Nibbles

by Emma R. Roberts

Photography by Ellen Callaway

ISBN 0-9786424-0-6

WIMMER
COOKBOOKS

Consolidated Graphics

Recipes For Success

2

Introduction

Every few years, I see a trend that really excites me. This is how I felt when we started promoting signature drinks to our clients and realized how much they embraced this new idea. There are so many possibilities for flavor, style, design, and creativity—the drinks began to set the tone for the entire event.

As we created these novel concoctions, I realized that harmonizing snacks were the perfect complement. Few people make their own snacks these days and the ones available at the market seemed to lack all sex appeal and any creativity. So... off we were on another creative adventure!

What a buzz these little nibbles created! I had never had so many requests for recipes as for these little morsels we created on a whim, almost as an afterthought. Our bars were crowded with snackers and additional bowls were required almost immediately.

The recipes in the book have been adapted for the home cook and embrace the same joie de vie without being too intimidating. By and large, the snacks can be made a day or so prior to your party and stored away in airtight containers. The drink components can be assembled with relative ease.

We hope you find these snacks and beverages to be as much fun as we think they are. The life of a party always lies in the tiniest of details! And it's these little items that people will always remember.

Happy entertaining!

Acknowledgements

Is any book truly a solitary effort? I hope not, as teamwork is the best and most enjoyable way to get any project done! I hope not, as teamwork is the best and most enjoyable way to get any project done! *Sassy Sips & Nibbles* pulled from the talents of many of our wonderful staff.

A big thank you is due Chuck Ray, mixologist extraordinaire and our General Manager, who mixed and remixed each of these drinks to perfection. A standing ovation goes to Deidre Antes, our Executive Chef, and Xyomie Padilla, our Executive Sous Chef, who both worked long hours tinkering with the concepts and ingredients that went into each of the delectable snacks. And, heartfelt thanks to the Capers team and our clients who volunteered as guinea pigs and provided thoughtful feedback on each recipe.

Jane Falla of Lisa Ekus Public Relations generously provided a wealth of knowledge into the finer points of cookbook publishing. I would have been lost without her gentle and wise counsel.

The Wimmer Cookbook team, especially Ardith Bradshaw and Maureen Fortune, spent hours on the design of this beautiful little book, and offered much needed moral support. They were able to keep us on time and on track!

Thank you to Jan Saragoni our PR guru who has helped to launch this book for us.

Lastly, a big thank you to my husband, Billy, for his constant support and patience. Without you, none of this could be possible.

Sips & Nibbles - Cocktails 101:

How to rim a glass:

Place rimming salt or sugar on a dish that is wider than the glass that you have chosen. Wipe the rim of the glass with a wedge of lemon or lime (you can also use water). Then invert the glass onto the dish and press gently. Lift the glass and shake off excess sugar or salt. This can be done to all glassware in advance and carefully set aside until needed.

How to chill a glass:

Rinse glass with cool water and store for several hours in the refrigerator.

How to insure a well chilled martini:

Store vodka and gin in the freezer.

How much ice do you need?

You should allow one pound per person per hour for a cocktail party serving mixed drinks. If the temperature is above 85 degrees, increase your ice order by 50%.

It is also necessary to have one 30-pound bag of ice per 2 cases of wine or beer to chill bottles down and keep them cold.

Ice can often be ordered from an ice company in volume and delivered directly to your home.

Liquor List for a 3 Hour Party for 50 Guests:

1-2 cases white wine

8 bottles red wine (this number depends upon your group)

2-4 liters vodka

2 liters gin

2-3 liters rum

1 liter Bourbon

1 liter whiskey

2 liters Scotch (depending on season)

1 small bottle dry vermouth

1 small bottle sweet vermouth

2 cases beer

½ case liter bottles of club soda

1 case liter bottles of tonic water

6 liters ginger ale

6 liters Diet Coke

6 liters Coke

1 case liter bottles of sparkling water

3 quarts orange juice

2 half-gallons cranberry juice

1 quart grapefruit juice

5 lemons

5 limes

Cocktail onion, cherries, olives, and caper berries (great for martinis)

What is the yield from different bottle sizes?

The following list is based on 1½ to 2 ounces of liquor per drink and half-filled 10-ounce wine glasses:

Fifth: 12-17 drinks

Quart: 16-21 drinks

Liter: 17-22 drinks

Half Gallon: 32-42 drinks

Gallon (liquor or wine): 75 drinks, 32 glasses

Wine Bottle: 6 glasses

Magnum (wine): 12 glasses

Champagne: 8-10 flutes

How many glasses do you need?

For a 3-hour cocktail party for 50 guests with a full bar you will need:

100 wine glasses	40 high balls	20 martini
40 low balls	25 pilsner	

If you have a signature beverage requiring a special glass, be sure to allow 1.25 glasses per person, or a total of approximately 65 glasses.

Renting glassware:

Unless you are a glassware addict, most hosts will need to rent when a party exceeds 20 guests.

Call caterers in your area to determine which rental companies are considered to be the best. Better rental companies will have a vast selection of glassware options. Visiting the rental company will give you the best idea of what your glassware options are.

Renting is a great way to create a look for one evening without making a substantial investment.

Making simple syrup:

Simple syrup is an integral part of many signature drinks and is easy to make:

Place 2 cups water and 2 cups sugar in a saucepan. Heat to a boil and boil for 5 minutes until sugar dissolves fully. Cool completely and store, covered, in a clean glass container. This keeps for weeks in the refrigerator and is perfect to have on hand to sweeten homemade iced tea and lemonade.

Where to put your bar:

You will need to view your house in a new way. I recommend walking through your front door with a pen and paper. Sketch the layout of your first floor and begin to think of your rooms as they might flow when filled with guests. You may want to note what furniture could be moved to improve the flow.

The best place to put a bar is in an open space that can be accessed from multiple directions and will be free of bottlenecking. Bay windows and corners of large rooms work well.

If entertaining more than 75 guests, you may want to consider utilizing two bar areas.

Table of Contents

Light my Fire (Winter Warmers)

Retro Classics

Wonton Frizzles with Love Potion

This passionate duo was created for a romantic bride who was married close to Valentine's Day. For a trio of romance, fill a silver Revere bowl full of Wonton Frizzles and add two more bowls—one of Red Hot Imperial Hearts and one of Necco Conversation Hearts.

Wonton Frizzles

Yield: 6 servings

1 **tablespoon finely ground sea salt**

1 **tablespoon Chinese five spice mix**

1 **tablespoon sugar**

½ **gallon peanut or vegetable oil**

1 **(16-ounce) package wonton wrappers**

In small bowl, combine salt, spice mix, and sugar; set aside. Heat oil in an electric fryer to 365 degrees. (Use candy thermometer to check temperature.) Evenly stack wrappers in sheets of ten. Cut squares into four smaller squares; then cut small squares into ¼-inch strips. Separate strips and carefully place in oil. Cook in small batches until crisp. Remove cooked strips from fryer and drain on paper towels. Sprinkle immediately with spice mixture. Cool completely and store in airtight container.

Wonton wrappers may be purchased in the produce section of larger supermarkets.

Sassy Sip Tip:

There is no need to purchase expensive champagne when mixing with other ingredients. Moderately priced sparkling wine works perfectly.

Love Potion

Yield: 6 servings

1 cup pomegranate juice
1 tablespoon superfine sugar
1 (1¼-inch) piece fresh ginger, thinly sliced
4 tablespoons orange juice
1 teaspoon Cointreau
1 (750-milliliter) bottle sparkling wine, chilled
1 pomegranate, seeded

Bring pomegranate juice, sugar, and ginger to a boil in heavy saucepan over medium-high heat, stirring often. Cook until mixture reduces to ⅓ cup. Allow to cool; strain mixture and discard ginger slices. Add orange juice and Cointreau to syrup, gently stirring. Pour 1 tablespoon syrup into each of 6 champagne flutes. Top off with sparkling wine and garnish with pomegranate seeds.

Syrup may be prepared a day in advance and stored in refrigerator.

11

Sassy Sip Tip:

We like to use Scharffen Berger chocolate for this recipe. To learn more about Scharffen Berger or to purchase their chocolate, go to www.scharffenberger.com. Any bittersweet chocolate will work.

Bittersweet Chocolate Ruffles with Not So Shirley Temple

We have a very special client who loves all chips. This zippy drink and elegant snack was served at her "Fiftieth Think Pink Birthday Extravaganza." These are also very popular with kids and have become a favorite of our Bar and Bat Mitzvah clients. Chocolate Ruffles are a quick and easy under-30-minutes snack!

Bittersweet Chocolate Ruffles

Yield: 8 to 10 servings

Slowly melt chocolate over medium heat in double boiler, stirring often. Dip chips in melted chocolate and coat halfway up. Transfer chips to parchment-lined baking sheet. Before chocolate hardens, sprinkle chocolate with sea salt. Allow chocolate to cool completely before serving. Serve in a silver Revere bowl or other elegant serving bowl.

1   **pound bittersweet chocolate, coarsely chopped**
1   **(12-ounce) bag Ruffles potato chips**
    Sea salt crystals

Chips are best the day prepared, but can be made hours in advance if the day is not humid. Carefully store chips in plastic airtight container, separating chip layers with parchment paper.

Not So Shirley Temple

Yield: 1 serving

Fill cocktail shaker with ice. Add Pimm's and next 3 ingredients; shake well and strain into ice-filled wine glass. Top with Prosecco and garnish with cucumber, strawberry, and mint leaves.

1½ **ounces Pimm's No. 1 Cup**
2   **ounces lemon juice**
1   **ounce simple syrup**
    Dash of grenadine
2-3 **ounces Prosecco (Italian sparkling wine), chilled**
2   **thin slices cucumber, skin removed**
1   **baby strawberry**
    Mint leaves

Smokey Cheese Arrows with Angel Punch

These were inspired by a ladies' spa party. Celebrate your inner angel and drink these while having a pedicure with your gal pals!

Smokey Cheese Arrows

Yield: 6 to 8 servings

½   **cup shredded smoked Gouda cheese**

½   **cup shredded Parmesan cheese**

1   **teaspoon cumin**

½   **teaspoon cayenne pepper**

1   **teaspoon ground coriander seed**

1   **teaspoon kosher salt**

1   **egg**

2   **tablespoons water**

1   **sheet frozen puff pastry, thawed as directed**

Preheat oven to 425 degrees. In small mixing bowl, combine cheeses and next 4 ingredients; set aside. In small bowl, combine egg and water; mix well and set aside. Roll out pastry sheet on floured surface to 16x10 inches. Cut in half to form two 8x10-inch rectangles. Brush one rectangle with egg wash and sprinkle with cheese mixture. Place remaining pastry on top of cheese pastry, pressing down to seal. Roll pastry to 8½x10½-inch sheet. Brush with egg wash; cut pastry with sharp knife or pizza cutter to ¾x8½-inch strips. Loosely twist pastry strip and arrange on baking sheet 1½ inches apart. Gently press twist ends to pan. Bake for 10 minutes or until golden brown. Transfer twists to baking rack to cool.

The driest champagne is brut, and a sweeter option is demi-sec. A sweet sparkling wine works well for Angel Punch. Purchase fun, flavored rimming sugars from www.cocktailcandy.com.

Yield: 1 serving

Pour nectar, wine, and grenadine into sugar rimmed champagne flute. Garnish with peach slice.

Angel Punch

- **1 ounce peach nectar**
- **5 ounces sparkling wine**
- **½ teaspoon grenadine**
- **Peach flavored rimming sugar**
- **1 pitted peach, halved and thinly sliced**

Cranberry cocktails are lovely when garnished with white or red cranberry swizzles. These can be made by skewering 4 to 5 cranberries on a toothpick or until toothpick is fully covered by cranberries. Red and white cranberries may also be alternated for a festive look.

Cheesy Cranberries with Cape Cod Kan-Kans

This cranberry snack was inspired by a recipe for "Cheesy Dates" given to us by a long-time client. We served these at a September wedding on a bluff in Cape Cod. We were excited to bring the flavors of the Cape into every aspect of the wedding.

Cheesy Cranberries

Yield: 6 to 8 servings

½ cup butter

2 cups shredded sharp Cheddar cheese

1 teaspoon salt

½ teaspoon cayenne pepper

1 cup all-purpose flour

½ teaspoon dry mustard

Dried cranberries

Preheat oven to 400 degrees. Melt butter and set aside to cool. In large mixing bowl, combine cheese and next 4 ingredients. Add butter to cheese mixture and mix well. Cover each cranberry with cheese dough to form small balls. Place cranberry balls on baking sheet and bake for 15 minutes or until browned. (The dough should cover approximately 40 to 50 cranberries.)

Cape Cod Kan-Kans

Yield: 1 serving

2 kumquats, thinly sliced
⅓ cup Grand Marnier
¼ cup superfine sugar
½ cup cranberry juice
1 (750-milliliter) bottle sparkling wine
Frozen, fresh cranberries

In large mixing bowl, combine 1 sliced kumquat, Grand Marnier, sugar, and juice. Using back of spoon, mash together ingredients and let stand for 5 minutes. Strain mixture through fine sieve over measuring cup, pressing on solids to extract all juice. In pitcher combine liquid kumquat mixture with sparkling wine. Pour into champagne flute and garnish with frozen cranberry swizzles (see Sassy Sip Tip) and slice of remaining kumquat.

17

Herbed Paris Puffs with a French Kiss

After watching the movie "Sabrina" with Audrey Hepburn, I was compelled to create something French. Share these with your significant other and spice up a summer evening!

Herbed Paris Puffs

Yield: 8 servings

¼	cup unsalted butter, cut into pieces
1	cup milk
2	tablespoons herbes de Provence
1	cup all-purpose flour
1	teaspoon salt
5	eggs
¾	cup finely shredded Parmesan cheese
¾	cup finely shredded Gruyère cheese

Preheat oven to 375 degrees. Combine butter and milk in medium saucepan. Bring to a boil over medium high heat. Remove from heat; add herbs, flour, and salt, mixing well until combined. Transfer saucepan back to heat, stirring until dough starts to pull away from pan sides. Remove from heat. Lightly beat 1 egg and fold into herbed mixture. Repeat process with each egg. Add cheeses and mix well. Line sheet pan with parchment paper and drop teaspoon-sized balls of dough on pan one inch apart. Bake for 15 to 20 minutes or until dough is golden brown.

French Kiss

Yield: 1 serving

1	ounce strawberry nectar
6	ounces chilled sparkling wine
1	strawberry, capped and thinly sliced

Pour nectar into coupe shaped champagne glass and add sparkling wine. Top with two strawberry slices, stem ends facing each other to form a kiss.

Sassy Sip Tip:

Don't toss leftover sparking wine—make vinaigrette! Combine together ½ cup extra virgin olive oil, ¼ cup champagne, ¼ cup champagne vinegar, a drop of honey, salt, and pepper. Sparkling wine also makes a wonderful poaching liquid for fish!

19

Coconut Puff Balls with a Cure for the Winter Blues

Coconut Puff Balls were created for a winter baby shower. These versatile snacks may be easily adapted to a dessert treat by using chocolate flavored crisped rice cereal. We have also made "truffles" out of them by dipping the balls into melted bittersweet chocolate and sprinkling with nuts.

Coconut Puff Balls

Yield: 6 to 8 servings

3 cups crisped rice cereal
½ cup unsweetened shredded coconut
2 tablespoons peanut butter
½ cup light corn syrup
2 teaspoons salt
¾ teaspoon cayenne pepper
1 tablespoon unsalted butter
2 tablespoons butter

In large mixing bowl, combine cereal and coconut; set aside. In heavy saucepan over medium heat, combine peanut butter and next 4 ingredients. Simmer, stirring until mixture comes to a boil. Remove from heat and pour over cereal mixture. Wash hands well and coat hands with butter. Form cereal mixture into 1-inch balls, working quickly before mixture hardens.

Coconut Puff Balls may be prepared ahead and crisped in oven on low temperature.

Cure for the Winter Blues

Yield: 4 to 6 servings

2   ruby red grapefruits, halved
½   cup superfine sugar
1   (750-milliliter) bottle sparkling
     wine, chilled
Pink rimming sugar

Juice grapefruits until 2 cups of juice are extracted. Combine juice, superfine sugar, and sparkling wine in a pitcher. Pour into champagne flutes rimmed with pink sugar and garnish with knotted peels (see Sassy Sip Tip).

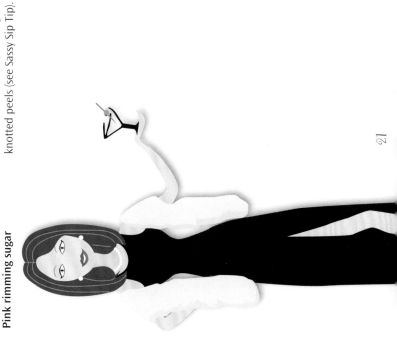

Upscale Trail Mix with Mount Katahdin Martinis

Instead of table numbers at a festive summer wedding, a bride and groom paid homage to the pastime that brought them together, hiking, and named each table after New England mountains. This idea sparked the inspiration for the following creations.

Upscale Trail Mix

Yield: 6 servings

¼ cup popcorn kernels
1 tablespoon cooking oil
¼ cup pecan halves
¼ cup hazelnuts
¼ cup small cashews
¼ cup dried blueberries or currants
½ cup pure maple syrup
¼ teaspoon ground ginger
¼ teaspoon cinnamon
½ teaspoon cayenne pepper
2 tablespoons butter
Salt to taste

Preheat oven to 350 degrees. Cook popcorn kernels in cooking oil according to package directions. Transfer popped corn to large bowl and set aside. Place nuts on three separate baking sheets and cook in oven for 6 to 8 minutes or until toasted. Remove from oven and let cool. Add nuts and dried fruit to popcorn bowl and set aside. In heavy saucepan over medium high heat, mix together syrup and next 4 ingredients. Simmer about 5 minutes. Slowly add syrup to popcorn mixture, stirring constantly. Transfer mixture to baking sheet and cool. Salt to taste and toss well before serving.

Mount Katahdin Martinis

Yield: 1 serving

1½ ounces premium vodka
2 ounces frozen Maine blueberries, puréed with 1 ounce water
¼ ounce freshly squeezed lime juice
Blueberry skewers
Fresh mint

Fill cocktail shaker with ice. Add vodka, blueberry purée, and lime juice; shake well and strain into martini glasses. Garnish with blueberry skewers and fresh mint.

Freezing berry skewers will help to keep your drink cold!

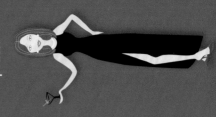

Citrus Spiced Mediterranean Olives with Lemon Ginger Twist

This cocktail was just one of five signature cocktails we developed for an "around-the-world" themed benefit. Each guest received a passport and took a culinary tour through multiple tents decorated to resemble the respective countries. We served this combination in the Tuscan-themed tent. After having their passports stamped at each destination, the guests entered a raffle to win an exotic trip.

Citrus Spiced Mediterranean Olives

Yield: 8 to 10 servings

1 pound high quality, mixed, brined olives

½ cup extra virgin olive oil

1 tablespoon minced garlic

2 teaspoons lemon zest

2 teaspoons orange zest

2 teaspoons cumin

1 tablespoon rosemary

2 teaspoons crushed red pepper flakes

2 teaspoons ground coriander seeds

2 teaspoons freshly ground pepper

Fresh herbs for garnish (optional)

Rinse olives in warm water, pat dry, and set aside. Heat oil in sauté pan over medium heat; add garlic and sauté 2 minutes, stirring well. Add zests and remaining ingredients, sautéing 2 additional minutes. Remove from heat and add olives. Return to heat and warm, gently stirring. Serve in bowls garnished with fresh herbs.

Warming the olives enhances the flavor!

These olives may be prepared several days in advance. Just reheat at 200 degrees for 15 minutes before serving.

Lemon Ginger Twist

Yield: 1 serving

1 lemon
2 ounces ginger brandy
2 ounces premium lemon vodka
1 tablespoon Ginger Sugar
 Lemon peel

Cut lemon in half. Quarter one half and set aside; juice remaining half and set aside. Fill cocktail shaker with ice. Add brandy, vodka, lemon juice, and Ginger Sugar; shake well and strain into chilled, sugar rimmed martini glasses. Garnish with curled lemon peel.

Ginger Sugar

1 cup sugar
5-8 pieces candied ginger
 (sold as crystallized ginger)

In food processor, combine sugar and candied ginger; pulse until finely ground. Rim martini glasses and place in refrigerator until ready to use.

Pickled Watermelon-Pepper Jack Bites with Mad Dog Beachtinis

Pickled Watermelon-Pepper Jack Bites

1 pound pepper-jack cheese

1 (10-ounce) jar pickled watermelon rind, drained

1 (12-ounce) jar sweet pickled red cherry peppers, drained

Yield: 4 to 6 servings

Cut cheese, rind, and peppers into ½-inch cubes. Thread cubes onto small decorative toothpicks and serve.

Mad Dog Beachtinis

Yield: 4 to 6 servings

1	watermelon
3	ounces sea salt and cracked pepper rimming salt
9	ounces rum
4	ounces freshly squeezed lime juice
3	ounces simple sugar syrup
6	lime wedges
6	thin watermelon slices

Cut watermelon into cubes, carefully removing seeds. In blender or food processor, pulse melon until puréed. (Add melon until 18 ounces of purée has been extracted.) Strain mixture through three or four cheesecloth layers, being sure to extract as much juice and as little pulp as possible. Chill large martini glasses by adding ice to the glass and topping with water; let stand 2 to 3 minutes. Remove and discard ice and water from glass. Rim martini glass with rimming salt. Fill cocktail shaker with ice. Add 1½ ounces vodka or rum, ½ ounce lime juice, ½ ounce simple sugar syrup, and 3 ounces watermelon purée; shake well and strain into prepared martini glass. Garnish with lime wedge and watermelon slice. Add a bright green straw cut to size (available at most party stores) for sipping.

Cigarettes with Black Orchids

A "Great Gatsby Roaring 20s Party" inspired these delectables. Imagine beaded flapper dresses, tuxedos, long strands of pearls tied in knots, and ladies "smoking" cigarettes with rhinestone encrusted 8-inch long black cigarette holders.

Yield: 6 to 8 servings

Sassy Sip Tip:

The "cigarettes" may be prepared with any smoked fish or no fish at all. We use premium vodkas in these drinks for the best results.

Cigarettes

4 ounces cream cheese, softened
1 anchovy filet
2 tablespoons grated Parmesan cheese
1 tablespoon chopped red onion
Salt and pepper to taste
1 (16-ounce) package 2½x2½-inch wonton wrappers
1 egg, beaten
2 cups cooking oil
Kosher salt

In food processor, combine cream cheese, anchovy, Parmesan cheese, onion; season with salt and pepper to taste. Pulse until well combined and set aside. Cut wonton wrappers in half and brush with beaten egg. Place ½ teaspoon cream cheese mixture down middle of wonton rectangle; seal wonton wrapper to form "cigarette." Place on parchment lined baking sheet. Repeat process with remaining wrappers and mixture. Transfer baking sheet to freezer for 2 hours. Heat oil in deep fryer until oil registers 365 degrees on oil or candy thermometer. Carefully place five "cigarettes" in hot oil and cook until golden brown. Remove from oil and place on paper towel lined plate. Sprinkle with kosher salt. Repeat process with remaining "cigarettes."

After freezing, these may be placed in plastic zip top bag for later use.

Black Orchid

Yield: 1 serving

Grape rimming sugar
- 2 ounces premium vodka
- ½ ounce Chambord
- ½ ounce blue curaçao
- 2 ounces cranberry juice
- 1 ounce freshly squeezed lime juice

Edible purple pansy

Rim martini glass with grape rimming sugar and chill. Fill cocktail shaker with ice. Add vodka, Chambord, curaçao, and juices; shake well and strain into martini glass. Garnish with edible purple pansy.

Coconut Rice Balls with a Green Tea Sake-tini

We passed this duet at an Asian wedding. We served the entrée in beautiful wooden bento boxes decorated with radishes cut in the bride's and groom's initials. This sake-tini is very light and refreshing and perfect for beginning a spring event.

Coconut Rice Balls

Yield: 6 to 8 servings

3	cups cooking oil
1½	cups cooked sticky rice
2	tablespoons white sesame seeds
1	cup grated, unsweetened coconut
1	tablespoon salt
3	eggs, beaten
	Kosher salt

Heat oil to 365 degrees in deep fryer. In large mixing bowl, combine rice, seeds, coconut, and salt. Shape into ½-inch balls and dip into beaten egg. Carefully place five balls into hot oil and cook until golden brown. Remove from oil and place on paper towel lined plate. Sprinkle with kosher salt. Repeat process with remaining balls.

These may be placed on a baking sheet and kept warm in low oven until ready to serve.

Sake-tinis are also perfect for serving in handmade cucumber cups. Cut a cucumber in 3-inch sections and form decorative stripes by peeling skin in ½-inch sections. Hollow out a 2½-inch section of seeds from each piece, leaving ½-inch layer of seeds on bottom, so sake-tini does not leak out of "cup." Pour sake-tini into decorative cucumber cups and serve to guests. Each cucumber should yield 3 to 4 mini-cups.

Green Tea Sake-tini

Yield: 1 serving

1 cup hot green tea, brewed according to package directions
1 tablespoon honey
2 ounces sake
Edible flower, such as orchid, for garnish

Combine hot tea and honey, stirring until honey dissolves. Allow to cool. Fill martini glass with ice and water and chill for 5 minutes. Remove and discard ice and water from martini glass. Fill cocktail shaker with ice. Add tea and sake, shaking vigorously until chilled, and strain into chilled martini glass. Garnish with flower.

Jimmy Carter Nibbles with Georgia on My Mind

We created this libation for a transplanted Southerner. We use peanuts from The Peanut Shop of Williamsburg (www.thepeanutshop.com). They are large plump peanuts that will make you consider doubling the batch!

Jimmy Carter Nibbles

Yield: 4 servings

½ cup peanuts
2 teaspoons salt
2 tablespoons sugar
¼ teaspoon cinnamon
¼ teaspoon cayenne pepper
¼ teaspoon ginger
3 tablespoons bourbon
½ teaspoon vanilla extract
½ teaspoon cayenne pepper
¼ cup molasses
1½ cups dry roasted peanuts

Preheat oven to 300 degrees. In food processor, combine ½ cup peanuts and next 5 ingredients; pulse until crumbled and set aside. In large mixing bowl, combine bourbon, vanilla, ½ teaspoon cayenne pepper, and molasses. Add peanuts, tossing well to coat. Place peanuts on baking sheet lined with parchment paper. Transfer to oven and roast for 7 minutes. Remove peanuts from oven, toss with reserved spice coating, and cool.

Sassy Sip Tip:

If any peanuts are left, try making this grilled peach dessert. Marinate peach halves in bourbon and grill until softened.

Top warm peaches with vanilla ice cream, sprinkle with chopped Jimmy Carter Nibbles, and serve immediately.

Georgia on My Mind

Yield: 1 serving

2½ **ounces premium vodka**
1 **ounce peach schnapps**
1 **ounce freshly squeezed orange juice**
1 **ounce peach nectar**
  Peach rimming sugar
1 **peach, pitted and thinly sliced**

Fill cocktail shaker with ice. Add vodka, schnapps, orange juice, and nectar; shake well. Rim martini glass with peach rimming sugar. Strain cocktail into chilled martini glass. Garnish with peach slice.

For Southern Punch, add 1 ounce of Southern Comfort.

Moon Rocks with Alien Seduction

One of our clients has an annual Halloween party, and each year she celebrates a letter of the alphabet. One year the letter was "M," and the guests came dressed as a variety of "M" characters, including Mork & Mindy, Madonna, Marilyn Monroe, Mr. T, Manny Ramirez (Go, Sox!), Molly Ringwald, a martian, a mummy, and many more. We made these Moon Rocks with an Alien Seduction for the occasion.

Moon Rocks

Yield: 8 to 10 servings

½   cup sugar
3   tablespoons kosher salt
       Freshly ground black pepper
2   cups honey
1   teaspoon orange zest
4   cups walnut halves

Preheat oven to 350 degrees. In large metal mixing bowl, combine sugar, salt, and pepper; set aside. Place baking rack atop sheet pan. Coat with nonstick cooking spray. In large, heavy saucepan over medium heat, simmer honey and zest for 3 minutes. Remove from heat and stir in walnuts in two batches. Remove coated walnuts on baking rack; bake for 6 to 10 minutes. Remove nuts from oven and transfer immediately to metal bowl, tossing well to coat in sugar mixture. Remove nuts from sugar mixture and cool on parchment lined baking sheet.

Nuts may be prepared several days in advance and stored in an airtight container. Be careful not to eat them all before the guests arrive!

Alien Seduction

Yield: 4 to 6 servings

1   cup vodka
1   cup Midori melon liqueur
1   cup Malibu coconut rum
3-4   cups pineapple juice
       Purple rimming sugar

In large pitcher, combine vodka, liqueur, rum, and juice. Rim martini glass with purple rimming sugar. Fill cocktail shaker with ice. Pour 6-8 ounces vodka mixture over ice, shaking vigorously. Strain into chilled, sugar rimmed martini glass.

Sassy Sip Tip:

If you are not making these Moon Rocks right away, store raw nuts in an airtight container kept in freezer to ensure they will not turn rancid. Freezing nuts promotes a longer shelf life. Moon Rocks are terrific in salads, too!

Sassy Sip Tip:

If you have an extra watermelon, why not spike it? Cut a round hole in the watermelon rind the size of the neck of the 750-milliliter vodka or light rum bottle you are planning to use. Invert the bottle into the hole and allow bottle to drain into the melon overnight. Chill watermelon until ready to serve and cut into small wedges. Serve the wedges on white summer platters garnished with fresh mint. Don't forget the light pink cocktail napkins!

Campfire Mini Biscuits with Jolly Rancher Cup

When we got a call from a casual bride and groom to be married in July on her family's farm, we were excited about all of the summer drink possibilities. When she mentioned that the groom was from the South, we decided to showcase the season's harvest with a hint of Dixie.

Campfire Mini Biscuits

Yield: 6 to 8 servings

½   **pound sharp Cheddar cheese, shredded**
½   **cup butter, melted**
1¼ **cups all-purpose flour**
½   **teaspoon dry mustard**
½   **teaspoon salt**
     Dash of cayenne pepper
5   **ounces cooked, ground chorizo (cold)**
1   **egg, beaten**
1   **tablespoon water**

In food processor, combine cheese and butter; pulse until blended and set aside. In mixing bowl, combine flour, mustard, salt, and pepper. Slowly add flour mixture to food processor and pulse well. Add cold chorizo, mixing well. Form dough into two balls, wrap each in plastic wrap, and chill overnight. Preheat oven to 350 degrees. Roll dough out to ½-inch thickness. Using ¼-inch cookie cutter, cut mini biscuits. Place biscuits on parchment paper lined baking sheet. In small bowl, combine egg and water; brush each biscuit with egg. Bake for 12 minutes until golden brown.

Biscuits may be prepared and baked a day ahead, then reheated. Store mini-biscuits in airtight container.

Jolly Rancher Cup

Yield: 4 servings

2   **cups seeded watermelon**
¼   **cup fresh mint**
2   **tablespoons lime juice**
2   **tablespoons superfine sugar**
4   **ounces premium watermelon vodka**
4   **watermelon slices**
4   **fresh mint sprigs**

In blender, combine watermelon, mint, lime juice, and sugar. Pulse until puréed; let stand 20 minutes. Strain watermelon mixture through fine mesh strainer and discard pulp. In pitcher, combine purée with vodka, gently stirring to combine. Pour into ice-filled punch cups and garnish with watermelon slices and fresh mint.

Lavash Snaps with Flip Flops

We crafted this combo for a rehearsal dinner we catered one late summer evening. The bridesmaids were given Dr. Scholl's sandals that were hand painted by the bride. The sandals were colorfully adorned with painted paper parasols and paired with matching nail polish–all bagged together in hot pink netting tied with pink bows.

Lavash Snaps

Yield: 6 to 8 servings

6	**sheets lavash bread**
½	**cup extra virgin olive oil**
½	**cup powdered milk**
½	**envelope dry onion soup mix**
¼	**teaspoon cayenne pepper**
1	**tablespoon chopped, fresh dill**
1	**tablespoon chopped, fresh parsley**
1	**tablespoon chopped, fresh sage**

Preheat oven to 350 degrees. Brush lavash bread with olive oil and set aside. In small mixing bowl, combine powdered milk, soup mix, and pepper. Sprinkle lavash bread with powdered milk mixture. Combine dill, parsley, and sage. Sprinkle lavash bread with herb mixture. Cut bread into 1-inch squares and bake for 8 minutes until crisp.

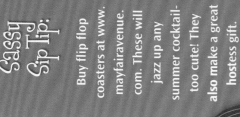

Buy flip flop coasters at www.mayfairavenue.com. These will jazz up any summer cocktail-too cute! They also make a great hostess gift.

Yield: 1 serving

In blender, purée raspberries with water. Fill cocktail shaker with ice and add purée, vodka, Cointreau, and lime juice. Shake vigorously until well blended. Pour mixture into martini glass and garnish with lemon twist and paper umbrella.

Flip Flops

1	ounce fresh raspberries
1	tablespoon water
3	ounces premium citrus vodka
½	ounce Cointreau
½	ounce freshly squeezed lime juice
	Lemon twists

It's always best to use acrylic martini glasses around a pool. We have purchased fun glasses for our clients at Target and Crate & Barrel stores. Look for festive polka-dotted glasses, too!

This Is Your Life Buoys with The Deep End

A 40th birthday pool party in July was the genesis of this combination. The entire party was coordinated in sea glass blues and greens–from the linens, to the cocktail napkins, to the serving platters. We focused on foods from the sea. Miniature lobster rolls, small row boats filled with ice and topped with oysters and littlenecks on the half-shell, swordfish kebobs with native corn and tomato compote, and Ipswich clam shooters were just a few of our gourmet delectables.

This Is Your Life Buoys

Yield: 6 servings

¼	**cup olive oil**
¼	**teaspoon garlic powder**
	Dash of cayenne pepper
1	**teaspoon ground oregano**
1	**tablespoon chili powder**
2	**teaspoons sea salt**
4	**cups Cheerios**

Preheat oven to 350 degrees. In small bowl, combine oil and next 5 ingredients. In large mixing bowl, toss Cheerios with oil mixture, coating well. Transfer mixture to baking sheet. Bake for 10 minutes until golden. Cool completely before serving.

Buoys may be prepared a day in advance and stored in airtight container.

The Deep End

Yield: 2 servings

6	**ounces premium vodka**
4	**ounces freshly squeezed lime juice**
1	**ounce blue Curaçao**
2	**teaspoons superfine sugar**
	Aqua blue rimming sugar
2	**lime slices, interior citrus removed**

Fill cocktail shaker with ice. Add vodka, lime juice, Curaçao, and sugar; shake well and strain into chilled martini glasses rimmed with aqua blue sugar. Garnish with hollowed lime slices.

Black Magic Tricks with Voodoo Potion

These were inspired by a Bourbon Street themed party. Be sure to purchase a lot of Mardi Gras beads; cook up some jambalaya, po' boys, and a King Cake; and dance until dawn.

Black Magic Tricks

2   cups Bugles
2   cups Corn Chex
2   cups Puffed Rice
2   cups Kix cereal
⅓   cup melted butter
2   tablespoons Creole or Cajun seasoning
2   teaspoons paprika
    Salt to taste

Yield: 8 to 10 servings

Preheat oven to 350 degrees. In large mixing bowl, combine Bugles, Corn Chex, Puffed Rice, and Kix cereal. Add melted butter and remaining ingredients, tossing well to coat. Place mixture on baking sheet and bake for 8 to 10 minutes, stirring occasionally.

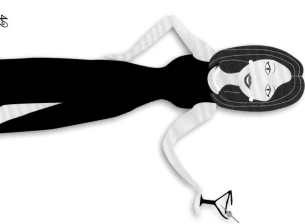

For invitations, send out masks made of light cardboard paper. Ask guests to decorate their own masks and have a group vote for the best mask. Winners receive Mardi Gras in-spired gifts, such as zydeco or jazz cds, a variety of hot sauces, cook-books, and more!

Voodoo Potion

Yield: 1 serving

1½ ounces light rum
1½ ounces dark rum
2   ounces freshly squeezed orange juice
1   ounce pineapple juice
1   ounce grenadine
     Orange slices
     Pineapple slices
     Maraschino cherries
     Sugar cane stalks
1   ounce 151 proof rum

Fill cocktail shaker with ice; add light and dark rums, juices, and grenadine. Shake vigorously and strain into tall Collins glass. Add fruit slices cherry and garnish with sugar cane stalk. Top off with remaining rum, and using a long lighter, ignite. Let burn until alcohol is burned off. Add skeleton straw and serve.

Skeleton straws are available at www.orientaltrading.com.

Spicy Curry Bites with Island Margaritas

This pair was created for a "Summer in Winter" themed party for a corporate client of ours. By late February, most New Englanders are all ready for a beach party. Build towers of varying sized blow-up beach balls, rent a life guard chair from a local prop company, and purchase some palm trees. Don't forget to play Jimmy Buffet, The Beach Boys, and reggae music!

Spicy Curry Bites

6 cups canola oil
1 tablespoon curry
2 tablespoons kosher salt
2 (12-ounce) packages 6-inch flour tortillas

Yield: 6 servings

In an electric fryer, heat oil to 365 degrees. In mixing bowl, combine curry and salt; set aside. Stack tortillas and cut into 8 wedges. Carefully place wedges in oil in batches and cook until crisp and lightly brown. Lift out with slotted spoon and transfer to parchment paper lined baking sheet. While hot, sprinkle wedges with curry mixture. Cool and serve.

Island Margaritas

Orange rimming salt

2 cups ice
4 ounces silver tequila
1 cup cubed mango
2 ounces Grand Marnier
2 ounces freshly squeezed
   lime juice
2 lime slices
2 mango slices
2 slices star fruit

Chill two margarita glasses and rim with orange salt. In blender, combine ice and next 5 ingredients; pulse until slushy. Pour mixture into glasses and garnish with fruits and cocktail monkeys.

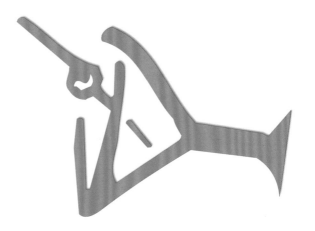

Girlfriend Nibbles with Provincetown Ritas

A summer bridal shower inspired these nibbles. They are wonderful eaten alone, dipped in lemon hummus, or with soup and a salad... truly a versatile creation!

Girlfriend Nibbles

Yield: 8 to 10 servings

2	**loaves focaccia bread, 1-inch thick**
½	**cup extra virgin olive oil**
1¼	**cups finely shredded sharp Cheddar cheese**
1	**tablespoon cumin**
1	**teaspoon cayenne pepper**
1	**tablespoon coriander**
1	**tablespoon chopped, fresh cilantro**
	Salt and pepper

Preheat oven to 350 degrees. Cut bread into 3½x½-inch pieces. In large mixing bowl, combine oil and remaining ingredients. Brush bread with oil mixture. Arrange bread on parchment paper lined baking sheet. Bake for 10 minutes. Turn bread over, brush with oil mixture, and bake until golden.

Provincetown Ritas

Yield: 1 serving

2 ounces premium gold tequila
1 ounce Cointreau
2 ounces freshly squeezed lime juice
1 ounce freshly squeezed orange juice
Light green rimming salt
1 lime wedge

Fill cocktail shaker with ice. Add tequila, Cointreau, and juices; shake well until chilled and combined. Pour into salt rimmed low-ball glass and garnish with lime wedge. Add a chili pepper straw and serve.

Chili pepper straws are available at www.orientaltrading.com. Straws are always a fun addition, especially in interesting colors and designs.

These straws are often too long for the glass you have chosen and may need to be customized by using scissors. Cutting a straw to the appropriate length can go a long way in solving the annoying problem of straws falling out of drinks!

47

In addition to Berry Mojitos, we served frozen banana daiquiris. Because we were at the beach with no power, we purchased a "Gator" for this beverage. The "Tailgator" is the most festive gadget I have come across in a long time. It's basically a "weed whacker" motor with a blender on top! To learn more about this fun item, visit www.totallygross.com. This gadget is also perfect for tailgating parties during football season!

Cuban Cabana Snacks with Berry Mojitos

A hot Latin beach party was the inspiration for these creations.

Cuban Cabana Snacks

Yield: 4 servings

1 medium sweet potato, peeled

1 medium yucca, peeled

1 medium plantain, peeled

1 Idaho potato, peeled

5 cups cooking oil

Salt to taste

Dash of cayenne pepper

Place peeled vegetables in water. Using small deep fryer, pour oil into fryer; heat to 365 degrees. Cut vegetables to 3-inch length. Set mandolin on fine julienne setting. Julienne vegetables and fry separately until crisp. Drain on paper towel. Sprinkle with salt and cayenne pepper.

Berry Mojitos

2-4 **fresh mint sprigs**
2 **teaspoons sugar**
1 **ounce freshly squeezed lime juice**
8 **fresh raspberries**
3 **ounces white rum**
  Club soda
  Crushed ice

Wash and stem mint leaves, reserving one sprig for garnish. Place mint leaves in bottom of glass and add sugar. Using back of spoon, press mint against glass, crushing well to extract mint oil. Add lime juice, raspberries, and rum, stirring until sugar dissolves. Add crushed ice and club soda to fill glass and gently stir. Garnish with reserved mint sprig.

Create decorative
ice cubes by
filling an ice
cube tray halfway
with water and
freezing. Add
sliced citrus fruit,
edible flowers,
fresh herbs, or
any small edible
item, then fill
tray completely
with water.

Freeze and store
decorative cubes
in plastic zip top
bag until ready
to use.

Pasta Swizzles with Summer Sizzles

These are one of the most dangerous snacks that we make! It's difficult to have enough for our clients, as we snap them up hot out of the oven. Serve them in tall silver mint julep glasses lined with parchment paper. They are also fantastic dipped in hummus or tapenade.

Pasta Swizzles

Yield: 6 to 8 servings

5   **fresh pasta sheets, available at www. pastacheese.com**

½   **cup extra virgin olive oil**

1   **cup shredded Pecorino Romano cheese**

2   **tablespoons chopped, fresh rosemary**

2   **tablespoons chopped, fresh thyme**

2   **tablespoons chopped, fresh parsley**

2   **tablespoons crushed red pepper**

    Salt and pepper to taste

Preheat oven to 425 degrees. Place pasta sheets on cutting board. Brush both sides of sheet with oil and sprinkle with cheese and remaining ingredients. Cut into 10x½-inch pieces and transfer to baking sheet. Bake for 5 minutes and remove from oven. Invert pasta pieces, return to oven, and bake for 3 minutes or until lightly brown and crispy. Serve immediately.

Sassy Sip Tip:

Ice cubes frozen in unique shapes and sizes add to a festive mood. Interesting ice cube tray shapes, such as stars, mini cubes, shells, and many more are available at www.fantes.com.

Summer Sizzle

8	ounces Goslings rum
5	ounces pineapple juice
5	ounces freshly squeezed orange juice
2	ounces grenadine
6	dashes angostura bitters
	Juice of 2 limes
	Pineapple rimming sugar
	Orange slices
	Maraschino cherries

Fill pitcher with crushed ice. Add rum and next 5 ingredients and stir. Pour into tall sugar rimmed Hurricane glasses. Garnish with orange slice, cherry, and hibiscus straw (available at www.orientaltrading.com).

51

Hens and Chicks in Paradise with Flamingo Rickey

These were created for a tailgating party prior to a Jimmy Buffet concert. We popped our tents and set up one mean barbecue... Mango Baby Back Ribs, Island Grilled Shrimp, Tropical Fruit Salad, and Chipotle Roasted New Potatoes spiced up the evening air. We even made S'mores laced with Coconut Fluff during intermission!

Hens and Chicks in Paradise

Yield: 8 to 10 servings

¾ **cup popcorn kernels**
2½ **tablespoons canola oil**
1 **cup chopped dried cherries**
2 **cups toasted, salted peanuts**
2⅔ **cups sugar**
½ **cup, plus 2 tablespoons light corn syrup**
½ **teaspoon salt**
1 **tablespoon white vinegar**
5 **drops pink or red food coloring**

Pop popcorn kernels in oil according to package directions. In large mixing bowl, combine popcorn, cherries, and nuts and set aside. In heavy saucepan over medium heat, combine sugar, corn syrup, salt, and vinegar. Heat mixture until candy thermometer registers 290 degrees. Add food coloring and mix well. Remove from heat and slowly pour over popcorn, mixing gently with wooden spoon to combine. Transfer mixture to parchment paper lined baking sheet coated with nonstick cooking spray. When cool, break into pieces and store in airtight container until ready to serve.

Flamingo straws are available at www.oriental-trading.com. If you don't want to use straws, serve these drinks with tiny plastic flamingos on the rim of each glass. We buy these at party stores, such as I-party and Party City.

Flamingo Rickey

Yield: 2 servings

Juice of ¼ lime
Pink rimming sugar

3 ounces premium vodka

2 cups lemon-lime flavored soda

3 ounces grenadine
Lime slice
Cherries

Rim tall glasses by rubbing edge with lime juice and dipping into pink rimming sugar. Fill two glasses with ice; pour vodka, soda, and grenadine equally between the glasses. Stir well to combine and garnish with lime slices, cherries, and flamingo straws.

Cheeszoos with Rose Sangria

Catering at the Franklin Park Zoo in Boston is always exciting. Our tent is usually located by the zebras, giraffes, and ostrich exhibits. The animals seem to have as much fun watching what we're doing as we have viewing them!

Cheeszoos

Yield: 6 to 8 servings

1	quart canola oil
1	(1-pound) polenta log, cut into ¼-inch slices
½	cup grated Parmesan cheese
2	cups all-purpose flour
1	teaspoon onion powder
2	tablespoons fresh, chopped parsley
	Salt and pepper to taste

Pour oil into deep fryer and heat to 365 degrees. Using small animal shaped cookie cutters, cut shapes from polenta slices and set aside. In large mixing bowl, combine cheese and remaining ingredients. Add polenta animals to cheese mixture, tossing well to coat. Carefully place 3 to 5 animals into deep fryer and cook until crisp. Repeat process until all animals are cooked. Drain on plate lined with paper towels. Sprinkle with additional salt if desired.

Rose Sangria

Yield: 6 servings

	Assorted melons
2	limes, thinly sliced
2	oranges, thinly sliced
1	ounce Cointreau
2	ounces brandy
2	tablespoons warm honey
1	(750-milliliter) bottle dry rose wine, chilled
6	ounces sparkling wine, chilled
½	cup edible rose petals (about 2 roses), gently rinsed

Cut melons to ¼-inch thickness. Using small animal shaped cookie cutters, cut shapes from melon slices. In large 2-quart glass pitcher, gently combine melon animals and next 5 ingredients. Carefully add rose wine and chill for 2 hours or overnight. When ready to serve, slowly add sparkling wine and rose petals, stirring gently with long handled spoon. Fill highball or wine glasses with ice cubes and slowly pour sangria over ice, allowing fruit and rose petals to enter glasses.

Asian Nuts with Shanghai Eggnog

I hosted a Chinese New Year party for my friends, and we produced this combination to start the evening off with a bang! A tradition was created of writing wishes on colorful crêpe paper and tossing them ceremoniously into my large, lit fireplace... hopefully, they came true!

Asian Nuts

Yield: 6 to 8 servings

- 1   tablespoon hot chili oil
- 1   tablespoon sugar
- 2   teaspoons curry
- 2   teaspoons garlic powder
- ¼   teaspoon five spice powder
- 3   cups dry roasted peanuts
- ¼   cup soy sauce
-      Salt to taste

Preheat oven to 350 degrees. Pour oil in large skillet over low heat. Add sugar, curry, garlic powder and five spice powder; heat for 1 minute. Add peanuts, coating well with spices. Add soy sauce and mix well. Transfer peanut mixture to baking sheet and bake for 20 minutes, stirring occasionally. Season with salt to taste if desired.

Sassy Sip Tip:

There are twelve Chinese zodiac animals (dog, dragon, horse, monkey, pig, ox, rabbit, rat, rooster, sheep, snake, and tiger) that create the cyclical nature of time. Consider incorporating an animal into your Chinese New Year celebration. My party kicked off the year of the "rooster."

I sent rooster invitations with Chinese characters, had rooster cocktail napkins designed, built roosters into the centerpieces, served ginger and five spice deviled eggs, and ended the evening with meringue bird's nests with baby chocolate eggs.

Shanghai Eggnog

Yield: 4 to 6 servings

1 cup sugar
½ cup water, separated
½ teaspoon lemon juice
6 eggs
4 cups milk
½ teaspoon vanilla
3 cinnamon sticks
3 star anise
6 (2-inch) pieces fresh gingerroot, sliced
6 cloves
6 black peppercorns
¾ cup heavy cream
2 tablespoons confectioners' sugar
1½ cups dark rum
Nutmeg or five spice powder

In medium saucepan over medium high heat, combine sugar, ¼ cup water, and lemon juice. Bring to boil; cook five minutes until mixture turns dark amber. Remove from heat and slowly stir in remaining ¼ cup water. In large mixing bowl, beat together eggs and milk. Add vanilla, cinnamon sticks, star anise, gingerroot, cloves, and peppercorns. Stir egg mixture into sugar mixture and cook over medium low heat about 10 minutes or until mixture thickens and coats back of spoon. Pour into pitcher and chill overnight. Before serving, strain mixture through fine mesh sieve and discard solids. In separate mixing bowl, beat together heavy cream and confectioners' sugar until soft peaks form. Pour rum and eggnog into punch bowl, top with whipped cream, and sprinkle with nutmeg or five spice powder.

57

Sweet and Hot Apple Chips with Hot Candied Apples

This combination is a perfect après-ski or served at a winter open house. Leave the Hot Candied Apples simmering on the stove as the guests arrive; it smells as wonderful and festive as a freshly baked apple pie.

Sweet and Hot Apple Chips

Yield: 6 to 8 servings

2 cups sugar
½ cup water
4 (2½-inch) firm MacIntosh apples
1 tablespoon kosher salt
½ teaspoon cinnamon
¼ teaspoon cayenne pepper
Dash of ground cloves

In heavy saucepan over medium heat, combine sugar and water; simmer until clear syrup forms. Using a mandolin, slice apples vertically through core into very thin slices. Dip slices into syrup and place on SILPAT lined baking sheet. In small mixing bowl, combine salt and remaining ingredients. Sprinkle apples with half of salt mixture and bake for 5 minutes. Remove from oven and turn slices over. Brush with remaining syrup and sprinkle with remaining salt mixture. Bake for additional 5 minutes until slices are golden brown.

Apple slices will keep for up to one week when stored in cool, dry area.

58

Hot Candied Apples

Yield: 4 servings

1 (36-ounce) bottle apple cider
9 ounces butterscotch Schnapps
3 cinnamon sticks
6 cloves
1 teaspoon nutmeg
Whipped cream topping, available in the dairy section of any supermarket
Cinnamon

In heavy stockpot over medium low heat, combine cider and next 4 ingredients. Simmer for 10 minutes. Ladle cider into mugs, top with whipped cream topping, and sprinkle with cinnamon.

Spiced Oyster Crackers with Fairwinds

A corporate team-building event was the origin for these snacks. We rented a Liberty Clipper Ship for our client, and a New England menu was in order, but also something easy to eat while the group hoisted the sails. We decided to serve Spiced Oyster Crackers on the bar (and in the soup), mugs of hot Clam Chowder with Fresh Dill, Baby Maine Lobster Rolls, and Mini-Ice Cream Cones. These were the perfect snacks for a day of sailing.

Spiced Oyster Crackers

Yield: 4 to 6 servings

1 **cup salted butter**

½ **cup Dijon mustard**

1 **(10-ounce) package oyster crackers**

½ **cup grated Parmesan cheese**

2 **tablespoons Old Bay Seasoning**

Preheat oven to 300 degrees. In small saucepan over medium heat, melt butter; add mustard, stirring well until combined. Place crackers in large bowl; pour butter over crackers, tossing well to coat. Add Parmesan and seasoning, tossing well again. Transfer crackers to parchment paper lined baking sheet. Bake for 5 minutes and stir. Bake an additional 5 minutes or until golden brown and dry.

Sassy Sip Tip:

Too busy to mix up your own Bloody Mary mixer? You can always purchase a fabulous one online at www.thevirginiacompany.com—it's called Sting Ray Bloody Mary Mix.

Fairwinds

Yield: 6 servings

- 4 tablespoons kosher salt
- 4 tablespoons freshly ground black pepper
- 2 teaspoons freshly minced rosemary
- 2 teaspoons freshly minced thyme
- 2 tablespoons celery seed
- 1 (36-ounce) bottle Bloody Mary mix
- 9 ounces vodka
- 4 tablespoons horseradish
- 1 tablespoon Dijon mustard
- 1 tablespoon Worcestershire sauce
- 4-6 dashes of Tabasco sauce

In medium mixing bowl, combine salt and next 4 ingredients. Set aside 2 tablespoons salt mixture for rimming glasses. Pour Bloody Mary mix into large pitcher. Add remaining salt mixture, vodka, and remaining ingredients; mix well to blend. Rim glasses with reserved salt mixture. Pour mixture over ice and serve immediately.

61

It's always important to remember that the tiniest detail is the difference between a party and an event. Events should be experiential and move through time with peaks of highlights throughout the evening-much like a successful Broadway play. The end of the night finale is just as important as the introduction- be sure to include a signature nightcap to your evening.

Chocolate Rods with Red Hots

For a holiday party we created chocolate moats-dark, white, and milk, in large rectangular vessels running down the middle of an eight-foot banquet table. Flanking the moat was a series of glass boxes filled with handmade marshmallows, crispy rice cereal treats, strawberries, baby bananas, biscotti, dried fruits, and pretzels. The pretzels were so popular that we customized a coffee bar with them!

Yield: 4 to 6 servings

Chocolate Rods

1   (8-ounce) package dark chocolate

1   (12-ounce) package thin pretzel sticks

    Kosher salt

2   ounces chocolate sprinkles

Melt chocolate in double boiler over medium high heat. Dip pretzel sticks in chocolate. Sprinkle salt and chocolate sprinkles on pretzel before chocolate dries. Place on parchment to dry before serving.

A coffee buffet is a festive way to end an evening. Place a large urn of coffee out with flavored syrups, whipped cream, shaved white and dark chocolate, cinnamon and cocoa powder shakers, rock sugar sticks, chocolate dipped teaspoons, after-dinner liqueurs, gourmet sugars, caramel, chocolate sprinkles, peppermint dust, and organic creams. Guests can create their own works of art. Don't forget to rent Irish coffee cups!

Red Hots

Yield: 1 serving

1½ ounces Irish cream
1   ounce Goldschlagger
8   ounces hot coffee or hot chocolate
1   **tablespoon whipped cream topping**

Combine Irish cream and Goldschlagger. Pour mixture into hot coffee or hot chocolate and top with whipped cream topping.

Sassy Sip Tip:

To avoid watering down a punch, always use 2 cups of a non-alcoholic and non-carbonated base liquid ingredient to make ice cubes.

Sweet & Salty Birdfeed with Harvest Punch

This festive punch was the brainchild of a "hoe-down" in a beautiful New England barn. We served the drink in small mason jars (any glass will do) and offered these snacks in open birdfeeders. These snacks also look terrific in small terracotta pots lined with parchment paper. If you don't own a birdfeeder or any gardening pots, small bowls work well, too.

Sweet & Salty Birdfeed

Yield: 8 servings

Preheat oven to 325 degrees. In skillet over medium heat, combine oil, honey, and cayenne; simmer for 2 minutes. In medium mixing bowl, combine seeds and coconut. Slowly incorporate seed mixture into honey mixture, mixing well until blended. Spread mixture over parchment paper lined sheet pan. Bake for 10-12 minutes. Remove from oven and season with salt. Crumble when cool. Store in airtight container until ready to serve.

- 2 tablespoons sesame oil
- ½ cup honey
-   Dash of cayenne pepper
- 2 cups hulled pumpkin seeds
- ½ cup sesame seeds
- ½ cup shredded coconut
-   Kosher salt

Harvest Punch

Yield: 8 servings

Pour 2 cups apple cider into ice cube molds and freeze. Pour 4 cups apple cider, club soda, Cointreau, and brandy into large punch bowl. Add apple cider ice cubes. Add sugar and stir vigorously. Float fruit slices on top.

- 6 cups apple cider, separated
- 1½ cups club soda
- 2 ounces Cointreau
- 4 ounces brandy
- ½ cup superfine sugar
- ½ crisp, red apple, thinly sliced
- ½ Bosc pear, thinly sliced
- ½ orange, thinly sliced in rounds

Pistachio Shortbread with Moose Mix

We are fortunate to have clients who like us to help them at their summer and winter homes. These treats were created for a post-holiday open house at a beautiful ski cabin in Vermont. We wanted something that said "warm and cozy" to the guests.

Pistachio Shortbread

Yield: 6 servings

1 **cup pistachio nuts, hulled**

¼ **cup all-purpose flour**

¼ **teaspoon salt**

Zest of 1 orange

1 **teaspoon cardamom**

3 **tablespoon unsalted butter, cut into pats**

¾ **cup grated manchego cheese**

¼ **cup grated Parmesan cheese**

¼ **cup sour cream**

In food processor, roughly chop nuts, then set aside. Combine flour, salt, zest, and cardamom in food processor. Add butter and pulse until crumbly. Slowly add cheeses and sour cream. Add nuts until just combined. Place mixture onto plastic wrap and form into 1⅓x10-inch log. Wrap in plastic wrap and freeze overnight. Preheat oven to 325 degrees. Remove plastic wrap from frozen log and slice into ½-inch circles. Place on baking sheet and bake for 6 minutes. Turn over circles and bake for additional 10-15 minutes until shortbreads are lightly brown and crisp.

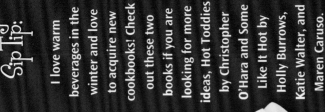

Sassy Sip Tip:

I love warm beverages in the winter and love to acquire new cookbooks! Check out these two books if you are looking for more ideas, Hot Toddies by Christopher O'Hara and Some Like It Hot by Holly Burrows, Katie Walter, and Maren Caruso.

Moose Mix

Yield: 4 servings

4	cups red wine
	Zest of 1 orange
4	cloves
	Seeds from 2 cardamom pods
1	cup aquavit
8	sugar cubes
	Blanched almonds, chopped
¼	cup golden raisins

In large saucepan over medium high heat, combine wine, zest, cloves, and seeds. Simmer for 10 minutes. In small saucepan over medium heat, bring aquavit to a simmer. Pour into wine mixture. Divide almonds and raisins among 4 serving mugs. Strain wine mixture and pour evenly into mugs.

Lucky Cowgirl Lassos with Pickled Dos Equis

These snacks were fashioned for a Southwestern Square Dance-inspired party. There were more calls the next day for the lasso recipe than there were for any other menu item that we had invented in months!

Lucky Cowgirl Lassos

Yield: 6 to 8 servings

1 quart canola oil

2½ cups all-purpose flour, separated

1 teaspoon cayenne pepper

1 tablespoon salt

4-5 medium Spanish onions, cut into ¼-inch rings

1 (1-ounce) package ranch dressing mix

1 egg, beaten

1 cup buttermilk

1½ tablespoons Tabasco sauce

3 cups panko (Japanese breadcrumbs)

Preheat oil in deep fryer to 365 degrees. In large mixing bowl, combine 2 cups flour, cayenne, and salt. Add onion rings, tossing well to coat, and set aside. In separate mixing bowl, combine remaining ½ cup flour, dressing mix, egg, buttermilk, and Tabasco and mix well. Dip onions into batter and dredge in panko. Deep fry until golden brown. Drain onion rings on paper towels and sprinkle with salt if desired.

Pickled Dos Equis

1   (12-ounce) bottle Dos Equis,
    extremely chilled
    Juice of ¼ lime
1   pickled jalapeño pepper

Yield: 1 serving

Pour beer into chilled pilsner glass. Add lime juice and **garnish with pepper.**

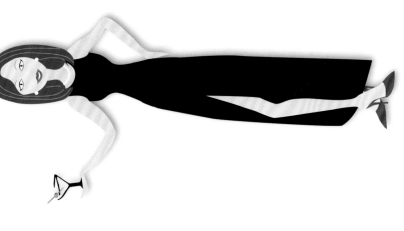

Cigars with Side Cars

"Ladies' Night" seems to have become de rigueur, but what about the gentlemen? One daring gentleman client decided he would have a "Men's Night" at his home, complete with martini bar, rare roast beef au jus, twice-baked potatoes, and fallen chocolate cakelets. From that thought, "Cigars with Side Cars" was born!

Cigars

4	**long Slim Jim sausages**
1	**cup finely grated Parmesan cheese**

Yield: 4 servings

Preheat oven to 350 degrees. Cut sausages in half lengthwise; cut each half into four pieces. Place Silpat* on baking sheet. Drop cheese onto Silpat* by tablespoons about 1½ inches apart. Bake for 3 to 5 minutes until cheese is lightly browned. Remove baking sheet from oven and place Silpat* on flat surface. Roll cheese discs around sausages and trim edges, forming a 3-inch "cigar." Transfer to serving plate and cool.

It is also festive to set up a self-serve gentlemen's martini bar filled with a variety of top-shelf vodkas, gins, mixers, and garnishes. Guests love to tailor their drinks and personally stylize their options. Check out our source guide for exciting martini companions.

Side Car

Yield: 1 serving

1½ ounces brandy
½ ounce Triple Sec
3 ounces sweet and sour mix
½ ounce freshly squeezed lime juice
Lime wedge

Fill cocktail shaker with ice. Add brandy, Triple Sec, sweet and sour mix, and lime juice. Shake vigorously until cold and pour into tall Collins glass. Garnish with lime wedge.

Delancy Street Bagel Noshes with Manhattans

A Manhattan themed Bat Mitzvah was the catalyst for these treats. We served the kids Serendipity-inspired Frozen Hot Chocolate (This recipe can be found in The Serendipity Cookbook by Pat Miller.) — not Manhattans! The room was lit with the skyline of "The Big Apple," and food stations included Zabar's on Broadway, Tao (as featured on "Sex and the City"), Dylan's candy bar, and more.

Delancy Street Bagel Noshes

Yield: 6 servings

- **6 plain mini bagels**
- **½ cup extra virgin olive oil**
- **2 tablespoons kosher salt**
- **2 teaspoons freshly ground black pepper**
- **¼ teaspoon cayenne pepper**
- **¼ teaspoon dry mustard**
- **2 teaspoons paprika**
- **½ cup grated Parmesan cheese**

Freeze bagels and slice as thinly as possible with bread knife, being careful not to cut yourself. Preheat oven to 325 degrees. Toss bagel slices in large bowl with olive oil. Arrange slices on baking sheet. In small bowl, combine salt and remaining ingredients. Sprinkle slices with half of seasoning mixture and bake for 8 minutes. Remove from oven, turn over, and sprinkle with remaining seasoning mixture. Bake an additional 8 minutes or until golden brown.

If possible, ask your local deli to slice the frozen bagels on their meat slicer!

Manhattan

Yield: 1 serving

¼ ounce sweet vermouth
2½ ounces Maker's Mark bourbon
    Dash of angostura bitters
    Maraschino cherries
1   **orange peel**

In mixing glass, combine vermouth, bourbon, and bitters with 2 to 3 large ice cubes, stirring gently. Place cherry in chilled cocktail glass and strain bourbon mixture over cherry. Rub cut edge of orange peel over rim of cocktail glass. Twist peel over drink to release oils, then discard peel. Serve cocktail chilled.

Bourbon Bites with Old-Fashioned

Book clubs are a great testing atmosphere for your drink recipes, old and new. Because it isn't a "party" and these groups promote opinions, you are bound to receive honest feedback. If you aren't a member of a book group, family and friends work well, too!

Bourbon Bites

4	cups pecan halves
2	cups bourbon
½	cup sugar
1	tablespoon ginger
1	tablespoon kosher salt
4	cups molasses

Soak pecans overnight in bourbon. Preheat oven to 350 degrees. In large mixing bowl, combine sugar, ginger, and salt; set aside. Place baking rack on baking sheet and coat with nonstick cooking spray. Drain pecans and pat dry on paper towels. In heavy saucepan, heat molasses over medium heat until bubbling; simmer for 3 minutes. Remove from heat and stir in nuts, coating well. Remove nuts from molasses with fork and transfer to baking rack. Bake nuts for 6 minutes; remove from oven. Add nuts immediately to sugar mixture, tossing well to keep nuts separated. Cool in single layer on parchment paper lined baking sheet.

Bourbon Bites keep for two weeks in cool, airtight container.

Bourbon Bites are addictive and should be eaten with caution! I always prepare a double-batch, as they are terrific given as hostess gifts, too. The best containers for gifts of food may be found at IKEA, Target, The Container Store, Crate & Barrel, and even the Christmas Tree Shop. Wrapping the nuts is half the fun!

Old-Fashioned

Yield: 1 serving

In old-fashioned glass, combine sugar cube, bitters, and water. Muddle well, add whiskey, and stir. Add lemon and lime twists and ice cubes. Add lemon and orange slices and top with cherry. Serve with swizzle stick.

1	sugar cube
	Dash of angostura bitters
1	teaspoon water
2	ounces blended whiskey
1	lemon peel twist
1	lime peel twist
1	lemon slice
1	orange slice
1	maraschino cherry

Sassy Sip Tip:

The richness of Pepperoni Quilts calls for a sour counterpoint, such as Whiskey Sour. Lemonade is also a wonderful match. Try creating a lemonade bar with Ginger-Mint Lemonade, Pink Watermelon Lemonade, and Limeade in large Mason jars with silver ladles... perfect for the summer, virgin or spiked!

Pepperoni Quilts with Whiskey Sours

These gems were created when we were looking for the flavor of "pigs-in-a-blanket," but wanted a more sophisticated upscale look.

Pepperoni Quilts

Yield: 6 to 8 servings

½ **pound sharp Cheddar cheese, shredded**

½ **cup butter, melted**

½ **teaspoon dry mustard**

Dash of cayenne pepper

1¼ **cups all-purpose flour**

½ **teaspoon salt**

1 **egg, beaten**

1 **(8-ounce) package sliced pepperoni**

In food processor, combine cheese and butter; pulse until blended and set aside. In large mixing bowl, combine mustard, pepper, flour, and salt. Slowly add flour mixture to cheese mixture in food processor, pulsing until well mixed. Shape dough into two balls and chill for 4 hours or overnight. Preheat oven to 350 degrees. Roll dough out to ¼-inch thickness. Using ¾-inch round cookie cutter, cut dough into circles. Brush rounds with beaten egg. Roll pepperoni slices into tight spirals and place into center of each round. Fold dough in half and pinch edges to form half-circle. Transfer to parchment lined baking sheet and chill for 30 minutes. Bake for 12 minutes or until golden brown.

Whiskey Sour

Yield: 1 serving

2 **ounces whiskey**

2 **tablespoons freshly squeezed lime juice**

½ **teaspoon powdered sugar**

1 **cherry**

½ **lime slice**

Fill cocktail shaker with ice. Add whiskey, lime juice, and sugar. Strain into low-ball glass filled with ice. Garnish with cherry and lime slice and serve chilled.

Pain Killer Clusters with Zombies

Pain Killer Clusters

Yield: 6 servings

We served the "Zombie" in ceramic coconut cups that I fell in love with at the restaurant Alma de Cuba in Philadelphia. My passion for this ceramic cup grew so great that we sent an employee to New York City to pick up 300 of them in Chinatown! It's always about "the look!"

1   **cup cooking oats**
½   **cup sliced almonds**
½   **cup pecans, chopped**
½   **cup salted peanuts, chopped**
¼   **cup white sesame seeds**
½   **cup sunflower seeds**
1   **cup light brown sugar**
½   **cup maple syrup**
½   **cup orange juice**
1   **teaspoon vanilla extract**
½   **teaspoon cayenne pepper**
¼   **teaspoon ground cloves**
¼   **cup butter, cut in pieces**

Preheat oven to 350 degrees. On parchment paper lined baking sheet, mix oats and next 5 ingredients. Bake for 10 minutes until toasted. Remove from oven and set aside. In heavy saucepan over medium high heat, combine brown sugar and next 5 ingredients, cooking until candy thermometer registers 290 degrees. Add butter, stirring well. Pour sugar mixture over nut mixture and mix well. Coat additional parchment paper with nonstick cooking spray and place over parchment paper to a heavy baking sheet over parchment paper. Place flatten nut mixture. Return to oven and bake for 6 minutes. Remove from oven and cool. When completely cool, break into pieces.

Sassy Sip Tip:

Think about starting a cocktail glass collection. So much of the fun in preparing a cocktail is wrapped up in the way the drink looks. Or become friends with your local party rental company–they may consider buying a certain glass pattern if you convince them that it will rent well!

Zombies

Yield: 1 serving

1 ounce light rum
¾ ounce crème de almond
½ ounce Triple Sec
1½ ounces sweet and sour mix
2 ounces freshly squeezed orange juice
3-4 ounces crushed ice
1 tablespoon 151 proof rum
1 cherry

In blender, combine rum and next 5 ingredients; purée until smooth. Pour into coconut cups and float 151 proof rum on top. Garnish with cherry attached to a palm tree toothpick (available at www.orientaltrading.com).

Signature Snacks and Cocktails –
Great Ideas and Resources

These ideas can be useful in personalizing your own creations.

To do:

1) Start a snack and cocktail binder. We use Staples mini-ring presentation binders to collect ideas that we create, as well as magazine pictures and recipes that inspire us. This gallery of ideas will move you to create your own unique ideas.

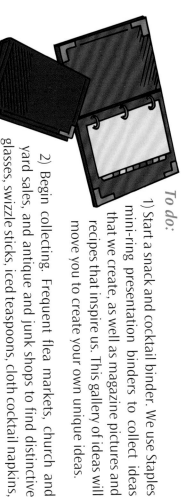

2) Begin collecting. Frequent flea markets, church and yard sales, and antique and junk shops to find distinctive glasses, swizzle sticks, iced teaspoons, cloth cocktail napkins, and more.

3) Keep an entertaining journal. Keep lists of the type of party you had, date, guests, seating arrangements, menu, and most importantly, what did and did not work. Trial and error are often the best teachers.

Garnishes and helpful hints:

4) Impale up to 6 cranberries on a toothpick to form a cranberry stirrer — this is the perfect garnish for any cranberry flavored cocktail.

5) Toothpicks can be impaled with blueberries too!

6) Use sprinkles / jimmies as a glass rimmer instead of the usual salts and sugars.

7) Use shaved chocolate as a glass rimmer — perfect for a Godiva chocolate martini.

8) Peel a cucumber, slice it into 2-inch pieces, and hollow out 1 inch of seeds. This creates an ideal "cup" for serving sake. Garnish with a julienned cucumber peel.

9) Candy barber poles make great stirrers for any drink (available at **www.hammondscandies.com**).

10) Hang plastic monkeys from the rim of any glass (available at **www.cocktailware.com**) to liven rum punches and frozen banana daiquiris.

11) Slice a honeydew melon thinly. Using alphabet cookie cutters, cut melon slices into the guest of honor's first initial. Float these monogrammed melons to personalize Provincetown Ritas.

12) Chill martini glasses. Using a commercial chocolate sauce that creates a shell, rim the glasses with chocolate sauce. Use the rimming method described in our Helpful Notes section.

13) Make your own swizzles. Buy clear plain swizzles at a party store and the game Sorry. Crazy glue the Sorry pieces onto the swizzle sticks and dry completely. These are perfect for a game night party. Dice are also fun to glue on.

14) Read Party Shots: Recipes for Jiggle-lscious Fun by Mittie Hellmich (available on **www.Amazon.com**), then create your own Jell-o shots. These can be cut into many shapes with small cookie cutters.

15) A gelatin cocktail kit is also available for beginners at **www.barsupply warehouse.com** and includes disposable cups and an informative book.

16) Fill an ice cube tray half way with water and freeze. Top with an edible flower, lemon twist, or fresh herb. Fill tray completely with water and freeze. Decorative ice cubes are festive in any drink.

17) Infuse whipped cream with flavored liqueur and top any warm beverage creatively.

18) A shaving of chocolate floats nicely atop whipped cream. Use a vegetable peeler to make chocolate curls.

19) Create a stencil or purchase one at an arts and craft store. Hold the stencil over a drink topped with whipped cream and shake cocoa or cinnamon through the stencil, decorating the whipped cream.

20) Pixie Stix dust is a wonderful rimmer for sweet and sour beverages such as Lemon Drops.

21) Purchase maraschino cherries in a variety of colors (available at **www.thesavvybar.com**). These add more zip than the standard red cherries.

22) Using a sharp paring knife, cut a large section of peel from a lemon, lime, or orange. Then cut the peel into little stars with a cookie cutter (available at

www.foosecookiecutters.com) or any other small shape. These shapes float well in any martini.

23) Try rimming the glass with celery salt when making Bloody Caesars.

24) Skewers of cherry tomatoes, miniature mozzarella balls, and fresh basil are perfect stirrers for a Bloody Mary and double as a snack.

25) Pickled asparagus and green beans (available at **www.pickledveggies.com**) are another alternative for Bloody Mary garnishes.

26) The best variety of toothpicks for garnishing any drink may be selected at **www.pickonus.com**. I enjoy using the knotted picks to dress a drink up. Try skewering a standard olive — it immediately looks more polished.

27) Invest in ice cube trays from **www.fantes.com** — penguins and evergreen trees for holiday drinks, stars for the New Year, dolphins and shells in the summer, and apples for fall. IKEA also has some excellent ice tray options.

28) Color water with food coloring and freeze for decorative ice cubes. You can also freeze juices, iced tea, coffee and lemonade for flavored, colored ice.

29) Caper berries are a fast and decorative garnish in martinis.

30) Pink flamingo stirrers (available at **www.uptownflamingo.com**) dress up our Flamingo Rickeys.

31) With a lemon peeler, peel long peels from the top to the bottom of a lemon. Tie these peels in a knot. You can also create these with limes and oranges. Add these to martinis or iced tea.

32) Start a glass collection by searching Ebay, flea markets, and yard sales. Concentrate on one variety of glass. It's not important that the glasses match, just that they are in the same genre. Silver mint julep glasses are particularly nice to own for mint juleps, as decorative containers for cheese straws, or for floral arrangements.

33) If you don't have silver mint julep glasses, use rocks glasses and garnish juleps with skewers of honeydew melon balls. Melon ball skewers can be made by using a petite melon baller, then threading 3-5 balls to a skewer.

34) Frozen grapes can be used instead of ice cubes.

35) Add cinnamon sticks to garnish punch glasses filled with Harvest Punch.

36) Neon flex straws add life to any pool party cocktail (available at **www.iparty.com**) and are perfect for Berry Mojitos.

37) Iced Tea Sippers in lemon, peppermint, and orange flavors are beautiful candy straws and are fun in any tall iced beverage. These are available at **www.hammondscandies.com**.

38) Make your own drink charms using decorative punches on card stock (both available at craft stores in the scrapbook department), beads, and thin wire for tying charms onto wine glass stems. Each guest's name can be written on the decorative paper tag. In the fall choose decorative leaf punches.

39) Try lighted blinking ice cubes in red, green, purple, blue, and white (available at **www.flashingblinkylights.com**) — you will need real ice, too, as these are merely decorative.

40) Garnish an appletini with thinly sliced lady apple rounds. Apple rounds can be made in advance and stored in cool lemon water to keep them from turning brown.

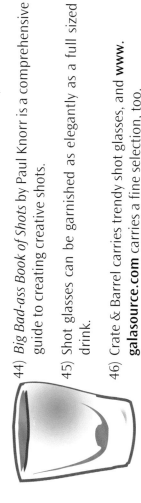

41) Appletinis and cider beverages can also be decorated with "Tini Apples," a very cute miniature apple (available at **www.cocktailware.com**).

42) Toasted coconut flakes can be pulsed in a food processor and used as a rimmer for piña coladas, rum punch, or any tropical beverage.

43) Colorful shots can be displayed and passed to guests in glass test tubes held in wooden test tube holders (available at **www.wardsci.com**).

44) *Big Bad-ass Book of Shots* by Paul Knorr is a comprehensive guide to creating creative shots.

45) Shot glasses can be garnished as elegantly as a full sized drink.

46) Crate & Barrel carries trendy shot glasses, and **www.galasource.com** carries a fine selection, too.

47) Keep your shots cold with shooter ice shot glasses. These fun ice molds create beautiful ice shot glasses (available at **www.worldwidefred.com**). These also are perfect for passing cold soups at cocktail parties.

48) Make your own infused vodkas to further flavor any drink. To learn more about this process visit **www.infused-vodka.com** for recipes and beautiful infused vodka containers.

49) Infuse your simple syrups by boiling herbs and fruits with your sugar water to enhance a drinks flavor. Strain and store in a clean glass jar and add fresh herbs and fruits for a decorative look.

50) Further dirty a martini by stuffing olives with blue cheese and skewering them to form a hearty swizzle. A drink and a snack in one!

51) Try artisan infused spirits by Boston chef Robert Fathman: Angelique tequila, and a bourbon and rum both called Diabolique, available to **Brix Wine Shop 617-542-2749**, in Boston.

52) Try New England micro vodkas from Maine's Cold River Vodka, Nantucket's Triple Eight Vodka, and Vermont's Spirits' Gold Vodka.

53) Make a decorative ice holder for bottles of vodka or gin by cutting off the top of an empty wax paper ½ gallon milk, putting the liquor bottle inside, and filling the container slowly with water freezing in layers. Add decorative herbs, flowers, fruits, and more and freeze in sections so that the decorations appear to be floating in the ice.

54) Using a citrus zester, zest lemons, limes, oranges, or grapefruits into long swirls by cutting/zesting along the circumference of the fruit. This gives each drink a festive swirl.

55) If you have your heart set on a signature drink, but lack the appropriate glassware for them, consider renting something fun from your local rental company. You will need 1.25 glasses per guest of the signature glass. Fill in with other glassware for soft drinks and beer.

Any Chinatown will yield a plethora of fun ideas — try these:

56) Scorpion bowls are terrific for rum punch. They are meant to be shared and are definitely an ice breaker. You can also purchase these at **www.tikifarm.com.**

57) Ten ounce ceramic coconut cups are a must-have for Mai Tais which should also be topped with paper umbrellas.

58) White ceramic sake cups can be used for warm sake and individual portions of snacks.

59) Custard straws are roughly twice the width of a standard straw and come in many fun colors. We especially like hot pink and bright green straws for summer drinks.

60) Asian tea cups are perfect for warm drinks like our Shanghai Eggnog.

61) Look out for decorative toothpicks — we buy ones with baby sea shells on top — these make pretty skewers for olives or onions in martinis.

62) Small Asian bamboo steamers display Wonton Frizzles or nuts at the bar.

63) Decorative chopsticks double as swizzle sticks.

64) Paper beverage umbrellas can be bought by the box and are much less expensive than at party stores.

65) Origami paper works well as a coaster and adds interest to Asian drinks.

66) Asian soup spoons are very inexpensive and are the perfect size for passing Jell-o shooters.

Wedding Ideas:

67) Bride & Groom Swizzle sticks of clear plastic topped with bridal veils and top hats are available at **www.foreverandalways.com**.

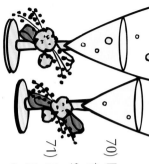

68) Kir royales of Chambord and sparkling wine can be garnished with pomegranate seeds instead of the classic raspberries.

69) Purchase jewel ice trays to make diamond ice cubes for your signature wedding drink (available at **www.worldwidefred.com**).

70) Make our kir royal sparkle like a jewel by dipping the rim of your glass into grenadine and then white sugar.

71) Design your own coasters and bring them to a local printer to be printed and cut. These are also a charming party favor.

72) Mason jars delightfully serve iced tea and lemonade and may be purchased at Target. Fill each jar with ice, lemon and lime rounds, and fresh herbs.

73) To make frozen lemon and lime rounds, place sliced lemons or limes in a muffin tin and fill one-quarter full with lemonade or water. Run tin under warm water to release decorative ice.

74) Create a decorative ice ring with a ring cake pan. Fill pan one-half full with water and freeze, then fill with fresh edible flowers and herbs. Top with water and freeze ring. Run ring under hot water to release the ice mold and float in a wedding punch, such as Harvest Punch.

75) Take the Pistachio Shortbread Dough and cut into wedding bells or hearts with a cookie cutter (available at **www.foosecookiecutters.com**).

76) Make your own colored rimming sugar by combining about ⅛ teaspoon powdered food coloring (available at **candylandcrafts.com** or baking supply stores) with 1 cup sugar in a mixing bowl until well combined. Store in an airtight container until ready to use.

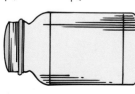

77) Pink or red organic rose petals float beautifully in rosé sparkling wine.

New Years Ideas:

78) Buy glitter sticks (available at **www.drinkstuff.com**) and use these to skewer olives, onions, or cherries in any martini or mixed drink.

79) Set up a champagne cocktail bar and allow guests to prepare their own creations. Set out cold champagne, orange juice, peach nectar, Chambord, rimming sugars, Demerara sugar cubes, and bowls of raspberries, strawberries, and orange half moons.

80) Create framed signs of champagne cocktail recipes to give guests new ideas to take home and use themselves.

81) Order an ice sculpture of a large martini glass — this is perfect for displaying, chilling champagne and vodka bottles, and starting terrific conversations.

82) Cut snowflakes out of white paper using a snowflake punch (available at craft stores). With a needle and clear thread, go through the edge of each snowflake and tie it onto the stem of each champagne glass.

83) Star fruit is the easiest of garnishes to make use of on a busy New Years evening.

Valentines:

84) Use red lollipops pulsed in a food processor (minus the stick!) for rimming glasses of Love Potion. Use other lollipop colors depending on the color of your drink — you can match or use complimentary colors.

85) Using red food coloring and water-filled heart shaped ice cube trays (available at **www.fantes.com**), float these ice cubes in any beverage you are serving.

86) Instead of the classic salty bar snack, purchase Valentine heart candy (available at **www.necco.com**) and watch conversations begin.

87) Serve Not-so-Shirley Temples garnished with organic, dark red rose petals.

88) Use elephant and donkey cookie cutters to make political party Cheeszoos.

89) American flag toothpicks (available at www. **abestkitchen.com**) are perfect for skewering olives, onions, cherries, or other garnish items.

90) Purchase animal glass hangers (available at **www.drinkstuff.com**), pick out the elephants and donkeys, and hang them from the rim of any beverage glass.

91) Use patriotic sprinkles (available at **www.foosecookiecutters. com**) to rim glasses with red, white, and blue and stars.

92) Garnish a Fourth of July sangria with red, clear, and blue star shaped ice cubes.

93) Purchase popsicle molds at your local supermarket (also available at **www.cooking.com**). Try making the following three alcoholic popsicles.

94) Piña Colada Popsicles: in a blender blend 3 cups pineapple chunks, ½ cup Parrot Bay Coconut Rum, and ½ cup canned cream of coconut. Pour into molds and add popsicle sticks. Freeze overnight.

95) Raspberry Margarita Popsicles: in a blender, blend 1½ pounds raspberrie ½ cup tequila, ½ cup sugar, and 2 tablespoons lime juice. Pour through a mesh strainer into a measuring cup and discard solids. Pour liquid into molds and add popsicle sticks. Freeze overnight.

96) Banana Daiquiri Popsicles: in a blender blend 3 cups sliced bananas, 6 tablespoons rum, ½ cup sugar, 4 tablespoons water, and 2 tablespoons lime juice. Pour into molds and add popsicle sticks. Freeze overnight.

97) Make white wine sangria and float fun melon shapes in each drink. Cut honeydew, cantaloupe, and watermelon into ¼ inch slices. Cut these slices into interesting shapes using small cookie cutters in the shapes of stars, the Statue of Liberty, the Liberty Bell, and flags.

Halloween:

98) Purchase acrylic crazy eye picks from **www.laprimashops.com** in pink flamingos, fish or lobster for fun drinks or for passed hors doeuvres. They are too cute!

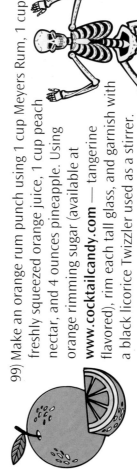

99) Make an orange rum punch using 1 cup Meyers Rum, 1 cup freshly squeezed orange juice, 1 cup peach nectar, and 4 ounces pineapple. Using orange rimming sugar (available at **www.cocktailcandy.com** — tangerine flavored), rim each tall glass, and garnish with a black licorice Twizzler used as a stirrer.

100) Buy gummy worms, available at most food or variety stores, and add these to each drink. These are particularly amusing in martini glasses.

101) Bendable skeletons (available at **www.rinovelty.com**) hang nicely from the rim of any glass.

102) Purchase 2-inch black plastic spiders (available at **www. rinovelty.com**) to float on the top of any festive drink.

103) Scary ice hands can be made with plastic disposable powder-free surgical gloves by filling each glove with water and tying the glove in a knot, much like a water balloon. When frozen, peel off glove and float hand in our Harvest Punch.

104) Hollow out large pumpkins and use them to hold bottles of beer and wine.

105) Place a small amount of dry ice in a large bowl and place a smaller punch bowl on top. This is a spooky way of serving a Halloween punch!

Holidays:

106) Pulse candy canes in the food processor. This is a great rimmer for the holiday season.

107) For the holidays, garnish peppermint martinis with miniature candy canes. These are available at most food or variety stores.

108) Purchase large red gumdrops, available at most grocery stores (also available at www.candyattic.com). Cut a slit in the bottom of the gumdrop with a paring knife and attach candy to the edge of any glass. This looks particularly festive when using a glass rimmed with sugar.

109) Purchase miniature holiday ornaments and ¼-inch red satin ribbon and tie them to the stem of each glass.

110) Purchase *Holiday Cocktails* by Jessica Strand (available at www.amazon.com) for additional fun ideas.

Other Fun Places to Shop for Accessories

Annie Glass
888-761-0050
www.annieglass.com
✳ glassware

Bar Supply Warehouse
2086 Afton
Houston, TX 77055
887-673-7676
www.barsupplywarehouse.com
✳ cocktail salt & sugar rimmer,
  gelatin cocktail kit, test tube kit

Boston Warehouse
59 Davis Avenue
Norwood, MA 02062
781-769-8550
www.bwtc.com
✳ old-fashioned glass swizzle sticks

Broadway Panhandler
477 Broome Street
New York, NY 10013
212-966-3434
www.broadwaypanhandler.com
✳ glassware, tableware

Catering Supplies
2638 SW 28th Lane
Coconut Grove, FL
305-443-0112
✳ Caspari napkins

Cocktailware
639 E. Broadway
Haverhill, MA 01930
978-556-6515
www.cocktailware.com
✳ swizzles, Tini apples, cocktail
  monkeys

Crate & Barrel
800-967-6696
www.crateandbarrel.com
✳ glassware, entertaining items

Dandelion Retail
55 Potrero Avenue
San Francisco, CA 94103
415-436-9200
www.tampopo.com
✳ glassware, serveware

Dansk
800-326-7528
www.dansk.com
* glassware, serveware

Fante's
1006 S. 9th Street
Philadelphia, PA 19147
www.fantes.com
* ice cube tray shapes: hearts,
starts, shells, penguin, miniatures
& more

Fishs Eddy
889 Broadway
New York, NY 10003
877-347-4733
www.fishseddy.com
* glassware, serveware

Franco's Cocktail Mixes
121 SW 5th Court
Pompano Beach, FL 33060-7909
800-782-4508
www.francoscocktailmixes.com
* rimming sugars and salts

Fred Cool Housewares & Gifts
Cumberland, RI 02864
1-866-801-5543
www.worldwidefred.com
* cool jewel ice trays, ice kebobs,
shooters ice shot glasses

Galasource, Inc.
3890 Elm Street
Denver, CO 80207
888-521-Gala
www.galasource.com
* frozen drink machines, glassware

glassybaby
435 NE 72nd Street
Seattle, WA 98115
206-568-7368
* cute colorful glasses

Global Table
107-109 Sullivan Street
New York, NY 10012
212-431-5839
www.globaltable.com
* glassware, serveware

Gucci
840 Madison Avenue
New York, NY 10021
www.gucci.com
✳ G ice cube trays

Hammond's Candies
5735 N. Washington Street
Denver, CO 80216
888-226-3999
www.hammondscandies.com
✳ candy canes, barber poles, iced
tea sipper straws

H.O. Foose Tinsmithing Co.
18 West Poplar Street
Fleetwood, PA 19522
610-944-1960
www.foosecookiecutters.com
✳ cookie cutters

iParty
800-447-2789
www.iparty.com
✳ swizzle sticks, paper parasols,
cocktail mermaids, cocktail
napkins

Mariposa
5 Elm Street
Manchester, MA
978-526-8132
✳ serveware

Nantucket Off-Shore
www.nantucketoffshore.com
✳ winter warmers

Off the Deep End
339 W. Antietam Street
Hagerstown, MD 21740
800-248-0645
www.islandmadness.com
✳ tiki ware

Oriental Trading Company, Inc.
800-875-8480
www.orientaltrading.com
✳ party supplies

Pearl River
477 Broadway
New York, NY
212-431-4770
www.pearlriver.com
✳ Asianware

Pier 1
800-245-4595
www.pier1.com
＊ glassware, serveware

Planet Sugar
800-950-8095
www.cocktailcandy.com
＊ rimming sugars

Pottery Barn
888-779-5176
www.potterybarn.com
＊ glassware

Quick Spice
323-728-4762
www.quickspice.com
＊ Asian items

Sable and Rosenfeld
131 Avenue Road, Suite 200
Toronto, Ontario M5R2H7
416-929-4214
www.sableandrosenfeld.com
＊ olives, onions

Savvy Bar
www.thesavvybar.com
＊ flavored cherries, glasses

Stirrings
508-324-9800
www.stirrings.com
＊ rimmers, mixers, and more!

Super 88 Market
50 Herald Street
Boston, MA 02118
617-423-1688
www.super88market.com
＊ Asianware, cool straws

Swank Martini Company
425 Jefferson Avenue
Toledo, OH 43604
866-487-9265
www.swankmartini.com
＊ glasses, drink accessories, frozen
alcoholic popsicle kit

Target
www.target.com
＊ glassware, swizzle sticks,
serveware

Tiki Farm
800-357-3360
www.tikifarm.com
＊ tikiware

Torani
800-775-1925
www.torani.com
✱ flavored syrups

Trader Vic's
P.O. Box 8603
1545 Park Avenue
Emeryvill, CA 94662
877-7-MAI-TAI
www.tradervics.com
✱ drink syrups

Williams-Sonoma
877-812-6235
www.williamssonoma.com
✱ salts, mixers, barware

Zak Designs
509-842-5377
www.laprimashops.com
✱ acrylic crazy eye picks in fish,
    lobsters, and pink famingo

*Flea markets are excellent places to find all
manner of glasses and interesting cocktail paraphernalia.*

Index

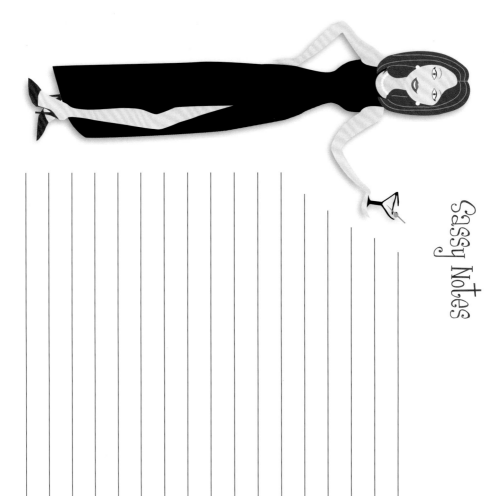

Sassy Notes

Sassy Notes

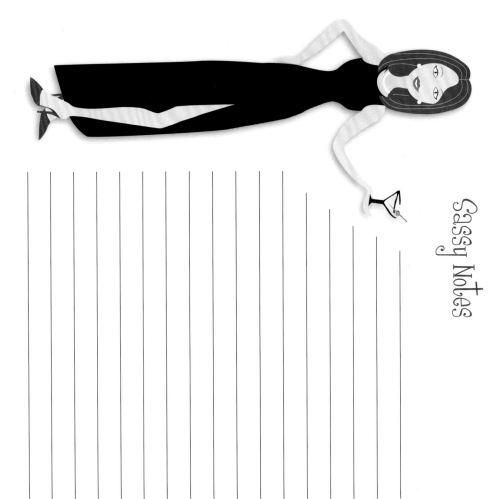

Sassy Notes

Sassy Sips & Nibbles

Capers Catering

21 Emerson Street, Stoneham, MA 02180

800-465-6509

www.caperscatering.com

Please send me _____ copies of Sassy Sips & Nibbles @ $15.95 each _____

Please add $6.00 shipping and handling for the first book and
$3.00 for each additional one to the same address $ _____

Massachusetts residents add 5% sales tax $ _____

                                                          TOTAL $ _____

Name _____

Address _____

City _____ State _____ Zip _____

Make checks payable to:
Capers Catering, Inc.

Please call for a credit card authorization form.

Sassy Sips & Nibbles

Capers Catering

21 Emerson Street, Stoneham, MA 02180

800-465-6509

www.caperscatering.com

Please send me _____ copies of Sassy Sips & Nibbles @ $15.95 each _____

Please add $6.00 shipping and handling for the first book and

$3.00 for each additional one to the same address $ _____

Massachusetts residents add 5% sales tax $ _____

                                                    TOTAL $ _____

Name _____

Address _____

City _____ State _____ Zip _____

Make checks payable to:
Capers Catering, Inc.

Please call for a credit card authorization form.